LIVE FROM THE CRYPT

Interview with the Ghost of

LOUIS PASTEUR

Series created by
David Salariya

Illustrated by
Rory Walker

Written by
John Townsend

BOOK HOUSE
a SALARIYA *imprint*

Meet the cast
TV crew:

STARRING MILLIONS OF MICROBES. MICROBES ARE TINY LIVING THINGS (MICROORGANISMS) WHICH ARE TOO SMALL TO BE SEEN WITH THE NAKED EYE, SUCH AS BACTERIA, VIRUSES AND SOME MOULDS (LIKE YEASTS). MOST MICROORGANISMS ARE ESSENTIAL TO LIFE ON EARTH. SOME CAN CAUSE DISEASE, AS DISCOVERED BY LOUIS PASTEUR.

MISH VARMA: HOST OF *LIVE FROM THE CRYPT* TV SHOW

JONTY YARDLEY: CO-HOST OF *LIVE FROM THE CRYPT* TV SHOW

LARNA OBATA: REPORTER

MANDY: HAIR & MAKE-UP

BINTI: DIRECTOR

KEV: CAMERA OPERATOR

ALEEMA: NEWSREADER

DUNCAN: SPECIAL CORRESPONDENT

GAIL FORSE: WEATHER PRESENTER

PROFESSOR LEPONT: A FRENCH SCIENTIST

Ghost Guests:

LOUIS PASTEUR (1822–1895): FRENCH SCIENTIST

MARIE PASTEUR (1826–1910): HIS WIFE AND SCIENCE ASSISTANT

MARIE LOUISE PASTEUR (1858–1934): THEIR DAUGHTER

EDWARD JENNER (1749–1823): BRITISH SCIENTIST

SARAH NELMES, MILKMAID, AND BLOSSOM THE COW FROM 1796

MADELEINE BRÈS (1842–1921): FIRST FRENCH WOMAN TO OBTAIN A MEDICAL DEGREE

FLORENCE NIGHTINGALE (1820–1910): BRITISH REFORMER OF NURSING AND HYGIENE

JOSEPH LISTER (1827–1912): BRITISH SURGEON AND A PIONEER OF ANTISEPTIC SURGERY

ÉMILE ROUX (1853–1933): FRENCH SCIENTIST AND COLLABORATOR OF LOUIS PASTEUR

ROBERT KOCH (1843–1910): GERMAN DOCTOR AND MICROBIOLOGIST

MAX VON PETTENKOFER (1818–1901): GERMAN CHEMIST AND HYGIENIST

JOHN SNOW (1813–1858): BRITISH DOCTOR AND HYGIENIST

ALEXANDER FLEMING (1881–1955): BRITISH MICROBIOLOGIST

Contents

Introduction

Just imagine it... the TV crew arrives in good time for a live broadcast on location in Paris.

They set up their equipment in an elegant brick and stone building on the Rue du Docteur Roux. Opened in 1887, this is the Pasteur Institute where amazing medical science has been going on for nearly 140 years.

In a private crypt below their former apartment, a famous scientist and his wife are buried. Their ghosts have never been interviewed on live TV before and the wonders of cutting-edge technology could just make this possible. And being cutting-edge experts themselves, how could their ghosts refuse the invitation?

What if the floor manager, tea boy, technicians, make-up team, reporters, presenters and director are all waiting nervously for a 'live encounter with the dead'?

What if we switch on at home for the TV show they said could never be done: *Live from the Crypt*?

Sit back and dare to be stunned...

Stand-by for lights, cameras, music —

ACTION...

Welcome to the programme

MISH:

Hello and welcome to another of our crypt programmes coming to you live...

JONTY:

With a few dead ingredients – in our new series *Live from the Crypt.*

MISH:

With Jonty Yardley and me, Mish Varma.

JONTY:

Your ghost-hunters searching for some of the most famous ghosts in history.

MISH:

And tonight, we've come to underground Paris to meet one of the nation's true heroes. Someone whose scientific discoveries have saved millions of lives.

JONTY:

Yes, we're at none other than The Pasteur Institute and down in the crypt beside an imposing tomb...

MISH:

In which lie the remains of two remarkable scientists – and maybe their ghosts.

JONTY:

So we're hoping to meet them LIVE and invite them onto our sofa.

MISH:

Yes, our set tonight has this glorious mosaic backdrop, as the whole ornate crypt is beautifully decorated with the achievements of Louis Pasteur, ably assisted by his wife, Marie. We have a comfy sofa waiting and we're inviting them to pop out for a friendly chat with Jonty and me.

JONTY:

Stunning though it is in here, it's a wonder why the great Louis Pasteur wasn't buried somewhere a bit grander.

MISH:

Then you obviously haven't done your homework, Jonty. He was first buried in the great Notre-Dame Cathedral.

JONTY:

Then he could have been badly scorched in the terrible fire there in 2019.

MISH:

Like I say, you haven't done your homework. Louis was taken from Notre-Dame shortly after his death and reburied here, even though the French government wanted him laid to rest in the Pantheon nearby, where many of the great people of France are buried. Marie Pasteur insisted her husband's resting place should be in his beloved Institute here. This crypt was once a cellar used as storage for medical equipment until it was crafted into this stunning crypt.

JONTY:

So let's take a look at some of the striking gold mosaics adorning the ceiling and walls, showing Louis Pasteur's great discoveries. There seem to be a lot of twisty plants and leaves and curly things.

MISH:

Those are tendrils, Jonty. Hops and grapevines. And over there are mulberry trees, speckled with silkworms and moths.

JONTY:

All very pretty, I suppose.

MISH:

If you'd done your homework, you'd know why they are so important.

JONTY:

What's the point of them, then?

MISH:

That's something you can ask Louis. Of course, I know the answer.

JONTY:

I suppose you know why there are chickens and countryside and sheep in fields in that mosaic?

MISH:

Of course – I've done my homework. Obviously,

you know why the pictures over there show dogs
and rabbits?

JONTY:

Obviously. Or if you're French, les chiens et les
lapins. See what I did there?

MISH:

You don't know why they're there, do you?

JONTY:

It looks like a growly dog chained to a stake whilst
two others look on. And there's a guy muzzling
a dog with a piece of rope. It must be to stop it
catching those white rabbits happily hopping in
a field.

MISH:

Wrong. Those rabbits and dogs changed the world –
thanks to Louis Pasteur.

JONTY:

Changed the world? That's going a bit far.

MISH:

No, really. Without them, we would be in fear and dread of viruses today.

JONTY:

Never heard of Coronavirus – Covid 19?

MISH:

Never heard of all the work on vaccines to get rid of it? Vaccine research continues in the labs just above us here. And it all started from the work of Louis – and Marie, his science assistant.

JONTY:

In that case, we need to talk to them. Shall I go over and knock on their tomb?

MISH:

No, Jonty – that's the job of our on-the-spot reporter who says she is ready to go.

JONTY:

Then let's go live to Larna, who is just behind us and hoping to meet the tomb's famous inhabitants.

MISH:

Yes, Jonty, the candles are lit and our special night-cameras are set up as midnight approaches – the time when ghosts are meant to stir and walk around.

JONTY:

I can't wait to hear them talk, even though my French is a bit rusty.

MISH:

No worries, a special app is fitted to our equipment to translate everything.

JONTY:

I can already hear in my earpiece that Larna is sensing a presence.

MISH:

Then we'll stop talking and let Larna see what develops, totally unscripted.

JONTY:

(whispering) So we now join Larna LIVE for 'No script at the crypt'. We're gripped!

No Script from the crypt

LARNA:

(*whispering*) Yes, Jonty, I'm here touching the tomb and I've given it a gentle knock. Is anyone in there? Can I have a little word, or as my app translates: Puis-je avoir un mot rapide?

VOICE:

Non – il ne souhaite pas être dérangé. In other words: he does not wish to be disturbed.

LARNA:

Is that Marie Pasteur speaking?

VOICE:

Well, it's not the Queen of Sheba, is it? What do you want?

LARNA:

We're *Live from the Crypt* and we're hoping to meet you and Monsieur Pasteur.

MARIE:

Professor Pasteur. He's busy right now. He's always busy.

LARNA:

Yes, I read that he once said, 'The only thing that can bring joy is work.'

MARIE:

I wasn't too pleased with that quote. He should have said, 'The only thing that can bring joy is work with my wife.' I had words with him about that.

LARNA:

What sort of words?

MARIE:

French ones. Now, leave us in peace...

LARNA:

We don't want to intrude but we wondered if Louis would...

MARIE:

Intruders have always been a problem. Hundreds came from miles around to get a cure for one thing and another. Everyone wanted to meet him and it was always me who had to warn him about overworking. With his own health problems, I had to be very firm. He needs to rest in peace.

LOUIS:

Who are you talking to, my dear?

MARIE:

Another intruder.

LOUIS:

Have they come for medical help?

LARNA:

No, just a chat about your life's work. We're hoping to bring along some of your past friends so you can discuss old times.

LOUIS:

That sounds interesting.

MARIE:

Which friends? I need to protect my husband from critics. Scientists sometimes mocked our work, until we proved our ideas were right.

LARNA:

We've asked your daughter to join us.

LOUIS:

Dear Marie Louise! How wonderful.

LARNA:

And Émile Roux, your old colleague. He really admires you.

LOUIS:

Then I'd better get myself tidy. How about it, Marie?

MARIE:

I'm not so sure. We don't want to catch any germs. I'll get some antiseptic.

LARNA:

By the way, I do like the famous photograph of you both together.

MARIE:

Pah! I hate it. Our daughter said I look too frumpy. That's because I had to stand so long without moving. We didn't do quick smiley photos back then.

LARNA:

You look as if you're a devoted couple.

MARIE:

We've been through a lot together. I'm very proud of Louis. He helped answer some of the biggest questions about deadly diseases. It wasn't easy.

LOUIS:

I think I'm ready to make an appearance. How do I look, Marie?

MARIE:

I'd better straighten your tie. I'll go out there with you to make sure they treat you with respect. It might be quite nice to get out and stretch our legs. We haven't been out much lately. There are so many germs about, you know.

LARNA:

We'll have a world exclusive interview! So whilst we wait for you to appear, it's back to Mish and Jonty on the sofa with their fingers firmly crossed...

MISH:

(Back on the sofa) It's sounding promising. And I've just heard we've got other guests on their way.

JONTY:

And they're all ghosts who long since passed away. Pasteur-way, get it?

MISH:

I think we should try to be respectful, Jonty. No inappropriate jokes.

JONTY:

Good idea, Mish. Then Louis might be keen to spook to us. See what I did there? So, before they join us here on the *Live from the Crypt* sofa, let's take a look at our plasma screen storyboard to remind us of the great scientist's start in life...

CUE THE FIRST VIDEO CLIP.

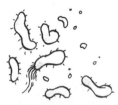

LIVE FROM THE CRYPT

The big bad wolf

LOUIS PASTEUR IS BORN IN THE WINTER OF 1822 IN A LITTLE HOUSE IN DOLE IN EASTERN FRANCE.

JOYEUX NOEL MON ENFANT, LOUIS.

MONSIEUR AND MADAME PASTEUR WELCOME THEIR NEW SON INTO THEIR HOME.

YOU'RE NO MORE THAN AVERAGE, BOY.

I CAN READ BECAUSE MY FATHER TAUGHT ME.

WE ARE NOT RICH BUT LOUIS WILL ALWAYS HAVE SHOES ON HIS FEET.

THAT'S BECAUSE YOU'RE A LEATHER WORKER, DEAR. BESIDES, HE WOULDN'T WEAR SHOES ANYWHERE ELSE, WOULD HE?

AT THE AGE OF 8, LOUIS GOES TO SCHOOL.

Interview with the Ghost of Louis Pasteur

IN OCTOBER 1831, A WILD WOLF WITH RABIES ATTACKS PEOPLE IN THE TOWN.

SACRE BLEU! WHAT IS THAT HORRID NOISE?

Behind the Scenes: the medical world of the 1830s

BINTI:

There's still no sign of Louis Pasteur's ghost. As the director, I'm in a panic. We won't have a programme if he doesn't show up anytime soon.

KEV:

The infrared camera isn't picking up any images around the tomb.

BINTI:

We'll have to go to a commercial break and get someone to dress up as the ghost. As you do hair and make-up, you could make yourself look like Marie Pasteur, Mandy.

MANDY:

(Offended) I look nothing like her! Anyway, wouldn't that be wrong?

BINTI:

You're right, Mandy, Kev will have to do it. Give him a beard, quick.

MANDY:

But Marie didn't have a beard.

KEV:

I can't be Louis. I can't act in French. Anyway, who would work the camera?

BINTI:

I will. No, better still, let's play for time. Bring in that professor of science we found upstairs. We'll do a feature about all the gruesome stuff around when

Louis was a kid. Meanwhile, tell Larna to get a move on. Hurry the ghosts!

MANDY:

They'll need some blusher and lippy or they'll look awful under the lights.

KEV:

They're ghosts, Mandy. Let them look natural... and scary. Yikes, I've just had a signal in my headphones. We've got ten seconds until our sofa goes live around the world.

BINTI:

Quick – Mish and Jonty stand by.

MISH:

What do we say?

KEV:

Seven seconds.

BINTI:

Make something up. Anything. Keep talking until someone shows up.

JONTY:

I can't waffle for long.

MISH:

You usually do.

KEV:

Three seconds... two... one...

MISH:

Welcome back to *Live From the Crypt* where we're beside the tomb of Louis Pasteur and Marie Pasteur.

JONTY:

And where, any minute now, we will be joined on the sofa by the Pasteurs themselves... just as soon as they appear. We hope. Possibly. Perhaps. Maybe.

MISH:

But in the meantime, we are joined by Professor Lepont, who lectures here at the Pasteur Institute on medicine and the history of diseases. Welcome.

Interview with the Ghost of Louis Pasteur

LEPONT

(Rushing on in bloodstained white coat) I wasn't expecting this. I'm in the middle of dissecting a body.

JONTY:

I wasn't expecting this, either... *(reacts to bloodstains, runs off about to be sick)*

MISH:

Professor Lepont, can you tell us what sort of world the young Louis Pasteur grew up in during the 1830s? How was medicine different then from today?

LEPONT:

Well, of course, doctors then had no real knowledge of how diseases spread. Hospitals were often filthy places full of germs. Safe operations were impossible and they didn't use anaesthetics. Going to hospital was a death sentence.

MISH:

So how was the young Louis affected by seeing rabies kill local people?

LEPONT:

He was suddenly aware of what a gruesome disease rabies was. One bite from an animal with rabies and you would eventually die a horrible death. Animals or people would froth at the mouth, lose control and go wild at the sight of water. Burning a bite-wound with a red-hot poker did no good at all.

MISH:

So the rabies germ gets into the bloodstream and attacks the body, right?

LEPONT:

Sure, it's a virus that infects the brain and nervous system. It takes several weeks or months for the symptoms to appear but by then it's too late. Thanks to Louis Pasteur, there is now a treatment if you get help in time. There's far less rabies around today than in his time but the virus is still out there.

JONTY:

(Returning but looking ill) Sorry about that, I'm a bit squeamish today. I hope you've finished talking about rabies?

Interview with the Ghost of Louis Pasteur

LEPONT:

All through history, there were all sorts of terrible treatments for rabies – none of them any good, of course. Things like viper's venom, crayfish eyes and the liver of a mad dog, minced up into disgusting, smelly medicines...

JONTY:

That's so gross... sorry about this... *(runs off, about to be sick)*

MISH:

I think Jonty might need some disinfectant wipes.

LEPONT:

Exactly. Thanks to Louis Pasteur, we're much more hygienic these days and know that diseases can be transmitted through bodily fluids, sneezing or tiny droplets in the air, as well as by being sick in a bucket behind the sofa.

MISH:

Didn't people used to think that they got sick from bad smells in the air?

LEPONT:

Exactly. Ever since the ancient Greeks, doctors believed in something called 'Miasma Theory', which said foul-smelling air was full of particles that could infect a body. They had no idea about microbes on our skin or up our noses, that could be left on surfaces for others to catch, coughed out from our mouths, left in toilets, or even carried by flies crawling over food or plates.

JONTY:

(Returning but looking more ill) Sorry about that... funny you should be talking about toilets. Can we discuss something else now?

LEPONT:

I can tell you what Louis Pasteur thought about smelly, festering flesh wounds...

JONTY:

No thanks... sorry about this... *(runs off, revolting noises)*

MINTY:

In that case, we'd better move on to our next item...
whatever it is.

BINTI:

(Through headphones) Go to another storyboard
or something. Where's Larna? Hurry up with the
ghosts! Where are they? And will someone get
Jonty's head out of that bucket?

KEV:

Cue next storyboard screen: three, two, one...

KEEP COUNTING...

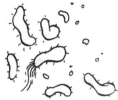

Off to Paris

Interview with the Ghost of Louis Pasteur

Commercial break

Live from the Crypt is brought to you by Killer Drinks Ltd and their new 'Death in a Glass' range of delicious drinks packed with deadly bacteria.

FOR CENTURIES PEOPLE HAVE BEEN GETTING SICK FROM DRINKING COLD OR WARM MILK, JUICES AND BREWS FULL OF FABULOUS FLAVOURS WRIGGLING WITH DIRTY LITTLE INVISIBLE DISEASES. JUST ONE SIP COULD BE ENOUGH TO PACK A TOXIC PUNCH.

SO WE AT KILLER DRINKS LTD ARE EXTENDING OUR RANGE TO INCLUDE KILLER FOODS AS A GUARANTEED NOXIOUS ACCOMPANIMENT TO ANY DEADLY DINNER PARTY. TRY OUR UNHYGIENIC EGGS AND CHEESES HEAVING WITH NOURISHMENT AND NASTINESS.

OUR POPULAR RAW PRODUCTS ARE ALIVE WITH SPECIAL INGREDIENTS SUCH AS TASTY TUBERCULOSIS, SCRUMPTIOUS SALMONELLA, DELICIOUS DIPHTHERIA, TANGY TYPHOID, CREAMY CHOLERA AND MANY MORE JUICY GERMS.

OUR SECRET RECIPES CONTAIN THE BEST LOCAL INGREDIENTS. WE ALWAYS LET OUR FRUIT FERMENT, FOR MAXIMUM FLAVOUR AND EXTRA BODY (OR BODIES). THEN WE CREATE A REFRESHING SUMMER DRINK TO DIE FOR, BUBBLING WITH BOTULISM.

OUR DELICIOUS FRESH MILK COMES STRAIGHT FROM THE COW, FULL OF NOURISHMENT, GOODNESS AND BOVINE TB, A MAJOR KILLER OF YOUNG CHILDREN IN THE 19TH CENTURY.

ENJOY!

STRAIGHT FROM THE COW.

DRINK AT YOUR OWN RISK.

WE JUST CAN'T STOP OUR PRODUCTS FROM CAUSING A SENSATION (AND VIOLENT ILLNESS). AVAILABLE FROM ALL GROSS STORES - GERMS AND CONDITIONS APPLY.

COMING SOON... KILLER KITTENS AND PERILOUS PUPPIES. OUR NEW DEADLY PET RANGE WILL INCLUDE CUTE LITTLE ANIMALS FULL OF RABIES. PLENTY OF FUN AND FROTH FOR ALL THE FAMILY.

WARNING: OUR FOOD, DRINKS AND PETS CAN HAVE DEADLY SIDE EFFECTS. ALWAYS READ THE LABEL. IT COULD BE THE LAST THING YOU READ. SURVIVAL NOT GUARANTEED.

Tough times

Interview with the Ghost of Louis Pasteur

Forecast

JONTY:

Whilst we're still waiting for Louis Pasteur to arrive, we can take a look at the latest forecast and get the outlook from Gail Forse. What sort of conditions could the Pasteurs expect, Gail? What might be coming their way?

GAIL:

A good question, Jonty. It looks like they're in for a lot of disease spreading across the region and not moving away for quite some time. Infections are setting in and sweeping across the area, with

severe blisters bubbling up in most parts. It will be extremely hot and feverish, with extreme conditions and little prospect of survival without major research.

All parts of the world are in for an especially stormy time with smallpox. This virus is among the most devastating illnesses ever suffered by humans. It has dramatically changed the course of human history and has even led to the decline of civilizations. It has often blown in with little warning.

Here's a quick look at some background. Smallpox probably started off in Africa, then spread to China and India thousands of years ago. The first recorded epidemic of smallpox was in Egypt, nearly three and a half thousand years ago. Almost two thousand years later this deadly disease reached Europe, where it swept through all countries from the fifth century to the twentieth century. From Europe the disease spread to major cities all around the world, including the Americas in the seventeenth and eighteenth centuries.

Interview with the Ghost of LOUIS PASTEUR

Throughout this time, smallpox accounted for hundreds of thousands of deaths each year and hundreds of millions in Louis Pasteur's lifetime.

Long before Louis Pasteur's birth, a king of his country died from smallpox. King Louis XV was cut by doctors who thought that bleeding would 'let out' the disease. Doctors had no idea how to treat smallpox until an English doctor came up with an amazing idea. He died the year after Louis was born, but both men made the forecast for human health much sunnier. Their work eventually sent smallpox packing. Dark smallpox clouds were blown away and the outlook is now very bright! And that's your forecast.

Through the Keyhole Surgery
TV game show – guess the home

DUNCAN:

Welcome to the game show 'Through the keyhole surgery', which features Larna Obata going around famous doctors' houses before asking a panel of historical celebrities to work out who the homeowner might be. As viewers probably know,

keyhole surgery is a modern technique of 'non-invasive' treatment, so we hope Larna will bear that in mind and not cause any damage as she enters, explores and shows us around the inside of this house. Then we'll meet our panel to see if they can spot the clues. Over to Larna's video...

LARNA:

I'm about to enter this beautiful Georgian house that stands in the English countryside. If you listen carefully, you might hear cows in the fields or the occasional cuckoo – both of great interest to the man who lived here. So let's step inside and note that a sign says, 'The Chantry'.

We can see a round working desk with a green top and a bookcase full of books about medicine and science, nature and hot air balloons. All around the rooms are tools and storage jars. Here is a pestle and mortar, knives and even some cow horns. Through the window, in the garden outside, is a work hut packed with medical paraphernalia, and a church behind is where our host is buried. His ghost has agreed to meet us later, when a taxi will take him to the studio.

By the way, just down the lane from here is a cottage that our celebrity gave to his gardener's son. Can you guess why? The young boy helped with some ground-breaking science that took place in this very room.

So let's recap the clues: an impressive home that was also a workplace, books that suggest education and research, plenty of tools and equipment that might suggest something surgical going on, dishes, needles and blades, masses of notebooks, papers and letters – and mounted on the wall are the horns of a cow, labelled 'Blossom'. So just what has been going on here?

Who would live in a house like this? It's now over to our guests to decide.

Back to you, Duncan.

DUNCAN:

Who, indeed, would live in a house like that? It's now time for our panel to decide. Let's meet them. First up is a famous medical campaigner who was a nurse in the Crimean War in the 1850s and has

done a lot to clean up hospitals ever since. She is
Florence Nightingale...

FLORENCE:

It's good to be here with some of my all-time
female heroes.

DUNCAN:

The one sitting next to you is none other than
Madeleine Brès, the first ever woman to become
a doctor in France, during the lifetime of Louis
Pasteur. And, like the great man, you did a lot for
child health and hygiene, didn't you?

MADELEINE:

Yes, and also like Louis Pasteur, I have a road
named after me in Paris. Unfortunately, mine is a
dead-end street!

DUNCAN:

And our third guest is none other than the fourth
child of Louis and Marie Pasteur. Please welcome
Marie Louise Pasteur, who outlived her parents as
well as Madeleine Brès.

MY 177TH BIRTHDAY IN 2019 WAS MARKED WITH A MADELEINE BRÈS GOOGLE LOGO!

MARIE LOUISE:

I'm a lot younger, after all. That means I've probably never heard of the owner of that house. It's in England, after all.

DUNCAN:

I think your father would have mentioned the owner, who was something of a hero of his. You could say that Louis followed in his footsteps.

FLORENCE:

In that case, I am guessing the person we are trying to find could have been a doctor in, say, the 1790s?

DUNCAN:

Correct.

MADELEINE:

During the French Revolution! It was a time of change everywhere, too. Was he, perhaps, seen as something of a crackpot by other doctors?

MARIE LOUISE:

My father was called that all the time because of his new ideas. People who challenge old beliefs often get insults. Now, I'm interested in this cow called Blossom. A cow, in French, is 'une vache'.

MADELEINE:

Of course, from the Latin 'vacca'.

FLORENCE:

Where we get our word 'vaccination' from.

DUNCAN:

Correct. Our mystery person coined the word 'vaccination' in that house.

MARIE LOUISE:

Larna told us about a gardener's son. Did our mystery person happen to do an experiment on a child, by any chance?

DUNCAN:

You're getting close.

FLORENCE:

I think the disease we might need to focus on could be smallpox.

DUNCAN:

Aha, now we're getting somewhere.

MADELEINE:

In my work, I was interested in how our bodies can sometimes fight diseases because of our immune system. The study of immunity is called immunology.

DUNCAN:

So who might be called 'The Father of Immunology'?

MARIE LOUISE:

Some people call my father that.

DUNCAN:

Then this must be 'The Grandfather of Immunology'.

FLORENCE:

I know who that is. I think I've got the answer!

DUNCAN:

Then go ahead and tell us whose house you think we've just seen.

FLORENCE:

Doctor Edward Jenner's.

DUNCAN:

Well done! And he's here right now, so please give a warm welcome to Edward Jenner...

Interview with the Ghost of Louis Pasteur

EDWARD:

(Entering to applause and sitting beside Duncan)
It's good to be with you.

DUNCAN:

And it's great to see you and your wonderful
house, Doctor Jenner. It's where you carried out
many experiments, I understand? Risky ones,
at that.

EDWARD:

Oh yes, I was always trying to discover what
made things work or what made people get
ill. Everyone remembers me for my risky work
on smallpox.

DUNCAN:

Indeed, and many years after your great vaccine
discovery in 1796, Louis Pasteur was so inspired by
you that he worked on vaccination in his lab, for all
sorts of diseases.

EDWARD:

I didn't have a proper science lab, just my study and
a hut in the garden.

DUNCAN:

And a cow. Tell us how you came up with your vaccination idea.

EDWARD:

Well, as you know, smallpox was a terrible, infectious killer disease. But an old country farmer's wife once told me she would never catch smallpox because she'd once caught cowpox from a cow. Cowpox isn't serious, it just causes a few days of blisters on the hands and that's about it.

DUNCAN:

Let me stop you there, as we've managed to find the ghost of Sarah. She was part of your story and she's just outside.

EDWARD:

Sarah Nelmes? Good heavens, I haven't seen her for years. We're all grateful to her, I can tell you. *(Sarah enters with a milking pail.)*

DUNCAN:

Welcome to Sarah Nelmes, the milkmaid who helped to change the world.

Interview with the Ghost of LOUIS PASTEUR

MY HANDS ARE STILL A BIT ITCHY.

SARAH:

I won't shake your hand just in case I've still got the cowpox. I caught it off Blossom, the cow. She's just outside, if you want to see her. Anyway, one morning I saw my hands were covered with blisters and I was horrified, so I ran up to the doctor's house, didn't I? I was in a proper flap, wasn't I?

EDWARD:

Yes, you were. You hammered on my door in a real panic.

SARAH:

'Doctor, doctor,' I cried, 'I think I've got deadly smallpox. Help.' I did, didn't I?

EDWARD:

You did. So I took a look at your hands and told you it was only cowpox.

SARAH:

I was so relieved. I can't tell you how much better I felt. That was until the doctor asked me a very odd question. 'Can I have some pus?' he said.

EDWARD:

That's right. I wanted to pop a blister and use some of the cowpox matter.

SARAH:

So that's what he did. One little pop and I was soon back to milking Blossom.

DUNCAN:

Good old Blossom. She helped to rid the world of smallpox.

SARAH:

Bless her. In fact she needs milking now, so I'd best be off. See you later, Doctor Jenner. I've brought you some nice milk, too. I've been milking all day and I'm up to my neck in full cream milk.

DUNCAN:

Pasteurised?

SARAH:

No, only up to my neck. See you! *(exits)*

DUNCAN:

I'm afraid our pasteurise joke won't mean anything yet, but stay with us. Firstly, do tell us, Doctor Jenner, what you did with the cowpox pus that you took from Sarah.

EDWARD:

I needed to demonstrate my theory on someone who hadn't been exposed to cows, smallpox or other diseases. A child. So I asked my gardener if I could use his eight-year-old son. I only wanted to infect him with a deadly disease!

DUNCAN:

Whatever did you do to him?

EDWARD:

Just a little scratch in his arm. Then I rubbed in the cowpox and waited. Little James Phipps developed mild cowpox but was right as rain in a few days.

DUNCAN:

I dread to think what's coming next.

EDWARD:

I needed to prove that if your body has a weak form of a disease, it is then able to fight off the deadly sort. So I rubbed some smallpox pus into James.

DUNCAN:

That must have been terrifying for him.

EDWARD:

Not really. I didn't bother him with all the grisly details. Besides, we didn't do risk assessments then. Anyway, it worked a treat. James didn't catch smallpox as my vaccination, as I called it, stopped him getting it. I galloped up to London to tell all the medical people what I'd proved.

DUNCAN:

Were they impressed?

EDWARD:

They said I was bonkers and sent me away. But after many years, I persuaded plenty of doctors to vaccinate people with cowpox to stop them from catching smallpox. Eventually the Royal College of Surgeons had to agree with me.

DUNCAN:

And eventually, with the work of others, like Louis Pasteur, vaccinations spread around the world and today there is no more smallpox out there. Around 1980 it disappeared forever.

EDWARD:

Really? How wonderful. I once said that I hoped someday that the practice of vaccination would spread all over the world, putting an end to smallpox, or the speckled monster, as I call it. So my dream came true – how wonderful!

DUNCAN

It took nearly 200 years since you first vaccinated James Phipps, but what an achievement. Louis Pasteur believed that if a vaccine could be found for smallpox, then a vaccine could be found for all diseases. So, some 80 years after your discovery, Pasteur was working on vaccines in Paris. And he, like you, took a huge risk by trying out a treatment on a child. But more of that later.

Interview with the Ghost of Louis Pasteur

EDWARD:

I can't wait to meet his ghost and have a jolly good chat about diseases.

DUNCAN:

We can't wait to meet him, either. That's if he ever shows up. But in the meantime, it just remains for me to say: Edward Jenner, thank you for talking to us, for inspiring scientists around the world and for letting us through the keyhole into your home. So, from all of us here, it's goodbye and back to the Louis Pasteur storyboard giant plasma screen...

I CAN'T WAIT TO SEE WHAT SCIENCE IS COMING NEXT.

In a nutshell

MISH:

Welcome back. We're still waiting for Louis Pasteur to appear. Apparently he's busy looking through his microscope and hunting for germs. So we'll go over to our special correspondent who has been given a real challenge tonight.

JONTY:

Yes, Duncan has the tricky task in *Live from the Crypt* to make a long subject as simple and short as possible – 'In a nutshell'.

MISH:

Not only does he have to keep us engaged, but he must also give us the basic facts in under a minute.

JONTY:

And as if that isn't tricky enough, Duncan has just been joined by Professor Lepont to explain some big science. Over to you, Duncan, and good luck...

DUNCAN:

Yes, welcome to 'In a Nutshell' and a special welcome to Professor Lepont.

LEPONT:

I'm happy to be back and to explain Louis Pasteur's big idea in a nutshell.

DUNCAN:

Fantastic – firstly, what did other scientists originally think caused diseases?

LEPONT:

Since the ancient Greeks, people often thought many diseases and even some creatures just appeared out of thin air. This was known as spontaneous generation. For example, a sack of grain left in a shed might soon have mice in it. Some people assumed the mice just emerged from inside the grain!

DUNCAN:

How weird. You only have 45 seconds left to make more sense.

LEPONT:

When a rotten piece of meat became full of maggots, it seemed like all those wriggly grubs appeared from nowhere if no one saw flies laying eggs on the meat. Some insects, like fleas, were thought to hatch out of dust. It was the same with disease, which was thought to appear by chance out of nothing. Louis Pasteur set out to prove that diseases came from microscopic 'germs' carried in the air. The idea of bacteria, viruses and fungi floating around, landing on surfaces and then infecting people just wasn't understood.

DUNCAN:

However did he prove that? Such microbes are just too small to be seen.

LEPONT:

In 1859, Pasteur disproved spontaneous generation when the Academy of Sciences sponsored a contest for the best experiment to prove it or otherwise. He demonstrated how tiny organisms in the air can cause disease and decay.

DUNCAN:

We'll show an image of what he did and maybe you can explain.

LEPONT:

Sure. Pasteur's winning experiment boiled meat broth in a flask. He heated the neck of the flask in a flame until it became soft enough to bend into an S shape. Air could enter the flask, but airborne microorganisms could not, as they got stuck in the bendy neck. As Pasteur had expected, no microorganisms got inside to grow and harm the broth.

When he tilted the flask so the broth made contact with the trapped airborne particles, the mixture soon became contaminated and 'cloudy with life' as it started to ferment. That's how Louis Pasteur proved that microorganisms are everywhere in the air and that tiny life doesn't just generate out of nowhere.

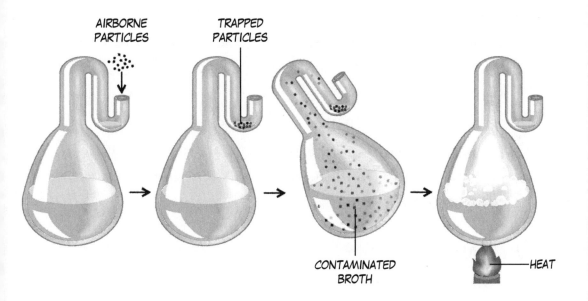

AIRBORNE PARTICLES

TRAPPED PARTICLES

CONTAMINATED BROTH

HEAT

DUNCAN:

Hey, that's clever. And I guess he then showed that heating the broth would kill the nasty microbes and make it safe to drink?

LEPONT:

That's about it. Liquids that are pasteurized will last much longer before spoiling.

83

DUNCAN:

So Louis Pasteur won the contest and changed what scientists thought.

LEPONT:

It took a long time before the world accepted his ideas, even though he received 2,500 francs for winning the contest. In fact, a French newspaper called *La Presse* printed: 'The experiments you quote, Monsieur Pasteur, will turn against you. The world into which you wish to take us is really too fantastic.'

DUNCAN:

Fantastic, indeed.

LEPONT:

Oui – c'est très fantastique!

DUNCAN:

I hope that has explained 'germ theory' in a nutshell within 60 seconds. That gives us enough time to go over to the French countryside and have a look around the farmyard – or should I say germ-yard? Here's a report from Gail...

Countryfail
(farmers with problems)

GAIL:

Welcome to 'Countryfail', the programme that reports on farming and environmental problems in the French countryside. Normally we would be meeting and talking to real French farmers but none of them wanted to be identified in case they'd never sell their diseased produce again, so their words will be spoken by actors... or by members of our crew, as they're cheaper. First up is a grape grower from the Champagne region...

BINTI:

I am furious. France is famous for champagne and my vineyards are the best in the world. I just sold hundreds of cases of wine to Britain but they sent it all back, complaining it was undrinkable. How dare they. Then I drank some myself and they're right. It's disgusting. What's gone wrong? What am I to do?

GAIL:

We'd better call in Professor Lepont to give us some advice.

LEPONT:

Simple. According to Louis Pasteur, harmful bacteria can cause wine to spoil. Heating wine to 50–60 degrees centigrade will get rid of that problem. But don't heat the grapes as they won't ferment then to make wine. Pasteur showed that the yeast needed to ferment grapes is found naturally in their skins. He demonstrated how sterilized grapes and grape juice on its own never ferments. Using sterilized needles to suck out the insides of the grape, he proved you can't make wine without the skins. No one knew that, so Louis Pasteur helped French farmers solve their problem.

Interview with the Ghost of LOUIS PASTEUR

GAIL:

We've now come to this hopfield to meet a farmer who grows hops for making beer. So what's failing in your business right now?

KEV:

I am furious. France is famous for making great beers and we compete with Germany to make the best. But now it's going down the drain – literally. For some reason, French beer has gone off. What's gone wrong? What am I to do?

GAIL:

We'd better call in Professor Lepont to give us some advice.

LEPONT:

Simple. Just like with wine, bacteria can attack the fermenting yeast and then it's undrinkable. In 1876 Pasteur published his book *Études sur la Bière (Studies on Beer)*. He described how yeast in the beer is often contaminated by bacteria, fungi and other yeasts. Because Germany had taken over the hop-growing region of Alsace-Lorraine after the 1870s Franco-Prussian war, Pasteur was

determined to improve the quality of French-made beers, to get back at Germany. By 'pasteurising' French beer and solving its diseased yeast problem, he said he'd make the 'Beer of National Revenge'.

GAIL:

So, once again, Louis Pasteur helped French farmers bounce back. But then chicken farmers had a big problem. What was killing off all their chickens? It's time to meet a poultry farmer who just isn't happy...

MANDY:

I am furious. France is famous for its cuisine and dishes like coq au vin and egg soufflé, but all my chickens are dropping off their perches and dying. I've only got one egg left – and please don't make any jokes that 'one egg is un oeuf'. It's disgusting. What's gone wrong? What am I to do?

GAIL:

You're not the only one losing flocks of chickens. So we've come to this poultry farm to ask Professor Lepont to give us some advice.

LEPONT:

Simple. The disease is chicken cholera. It can be a highly contagious and fatal epidemic that affects poultry farms. Louis Pasteur found it was caused by a 'germ' – a particular type of bacteria. Hey presto, he and his team got to work on a vaccine – more on that story later. Enough to say, problem solved. So once again, Louis Pasteur helped French farmers bounce back.

GAIL:

Now here's an amazing fact. The important French silk industry depends on farmers growing mulberry leaves. The highest quality silk comes from silkworms, which are caterpillars of silk moths fed on mulberry leaves. The French town of Lyon was a centre of Europe's silk industry. By 1870, Lyon had about 100,000 looms making silk cloth. They all needed a lot of silkworms to keep them busy. But disaster struck. Here's a silk farmer who just isn't happy...

DUNCAN:

I am furious. France is famous for its beautiful silks. All my silkworms are suddenly covered in

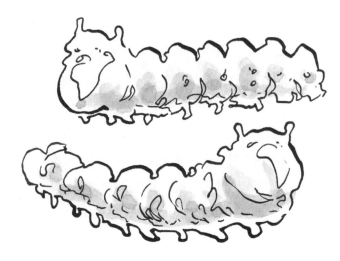

little black spots. Then they shrivel up and die. It's the same everywhere – no more silk. What's gone wrong? What am I to do?

GAIL:

We'd better call in Professor Lepont to give us some advice.

LEPONT:

Simple. Nasty little microorganisms infect the silkworms. This disease once caused an epidemic, killing the caterpillars and disrupting the whole French silk industry. Along came Louis Pasteur with his microscope and he identified the microbes causing all the trouble. Then he got busy to bring back healthy silkworms... more on that story later. Enough to say, problem solved. So once again, Louis Pasteur helped French farmers bounce back.

GAIL:

French farmers with cattle and sheep are next on the list. Here's a sheep farmer who just isn't happy...

ALEEMA:

I am furious. France is famous for its wool and mutton. But suddenly all my sheep are dropping like flies. They get a high fever and drop dead, with blood on their nose and mouth. What's gone wrong? What am I to do?

GAIL:

We'd better call in Professor Lepont to give us some advice.

LEPONT:

Simple. The disease is called anthrax. It's a nasty disease that can kill humans, too. Anthrax bacteria can be found in soil and may infect domestic and wild animals around the world. Sometimes epidemics can strike.

GAIL:

So what is the difference between bacteria and viruses, Professor Lepont?

LEPONT:

Good question. The study of viruses began when Pasteur died, at the very end of the 19th century. Although he and Edward Jenner developed the first vaccines to protect against viral infections, neither man knew viruses existed. Viruses weren't visible under their microscopes. Unlike bacteria, which are living organisms found everywhere, viruses are far smaller and are no more than a tiny genetic code that must invade living cells to grow and spread.

GAIL:

So what happened with Louis Pasteur and the dreaded anthrax?

LEPONT:

He worked on a vaccine – but more on that story later. Enough to say, problem now solved. Once again, Louis Pasteur helped French farmers bounce back. Bravo, Louis!

GAIL:

Amazing. So it's thanks to Louis Pasteur that this episode of 'Countryfail' turns into one of country success. Let's now examine those silkworms and the story from 1865, as we take another look at the storyboard giant plasma screen...

GET READY FOR THE NEXT STORY!

As smooth as Silk

WHEN TINY CATERPILLARS HATCH FROM SILK-MOTH EGGS, THEY FEED ON MULBERRY LEAVES.

SOON THEY SPIN SILKY COCOONS AROUND THEMSELVES.

Forecast
(cholera)

JONTY:

We're STILL waiting for Louis Pasteur to arrive on our sofa, so maybe whilst we keep trying to find him, we can go back to Gail Forse for a forecast update. What sort of conditions might we expect coming our way further ahead? Anything nice on the horizon?

GAIL:

I'm afraid not, Jonty. Dark clouds of disease are brewing, I'm afraid. You could even say things are turning FOWL because chickens are in for a grim time. Just to let you know, chicken cholera is a highly contagious disease caused by bacteria called Pasteurella multocida, so maybe you can guess who identified it, gave it a name and made a vaccine?

Human cholera is a related disease and can be just as deadly. When Louis Pasteur was a boy, pandemics spread across Europe, killing thousands of people in France. In 1853–54, an epidemic in London claimed over 10,000 lives, with 23,000 deaths throughout Great Britain. People became violently sick so much that they dehydrated and died after a few hours.

You will be pleased to know that the forecast is now much sunnier, after scientists like Louis Pasteur understood how such diseases spread and how good hygiene can act like an umbrella to protect you from infection.

As for the long-term forecast... cholera tends to die down after treatment these days and the outlook is now much brighter. And that's your forecast.

How nice to meet you

MISH:

Welcome back to the *Live from the Crypt* sofa with me, Mish Varma.

JONTY:

And me, Jonty Yardley – and we're very excited, aren't we, Mish?

MISH:

Excited and privileged because finally, at last, our special guests tonight have just arrived on set and will be joining us on the sofa any minute now.

JONTY:

Yes, the ghosts of Louis Pasteur and Marie Pasteur have appeared beside us and are just putting on their facemasks.

MISH:

Yes, the reason we're a little late meeting them is that we've had to disinfect the sofa and provide personal protective equipment as our guests are very concerned about hygiene.

MARIE:

It's not only that. Louis has been up to his neck in beetroot juice. He likes to re-check his theories about fermentation and alcohol. Come along, dear...

LOUIS:

You can never be too careful with all these germs about. Nasty little things, they are. You can only see them under a strong microscope. No one knew about them before my time. You must have plenty on your shoes, they're dirty. *(Sprays Jonty's shoes.)* I bet your feet are swarming with millions of microbes.

JONTY:

Come to think of it, my socks are a bit smelly.

LOUIS:

You must be gyrating with germs and fermenting with fungi.

MARIE:

Don't get him started. All his life, Louis tried to convince everyone they could catch diseases not just from airborne microbes, but from contaminated surfaces, moisture, droplets in sneezes, shaking hands...

LOUIS:

No one believed me at first. Doctors laughed at me when I told them that food and drink could be contaminated with harmful microbes, to say nothing of equipment in hospitals. You just touched your mouth – not a good idea.

MISH:

Sorry, I wasn't thinking.

LOUIS:

When did you last wash your hands with soap and hot water?

MISH:

Erm... I'm not sure.

MARIE:

Louis has a saying, don't you, dear?

LOUIS:

I have several. Lavez-vous les mains.

JONTY :

Wash your hands. Even I know that!

MARIE:

Be aware, wash with care.

JONTY:

Don't lick, germs stick. If you cough, wash them off!

MISH:

That's enough, Jonty. Tell me, Professor Pasteur, what would you say was your greatest achievement?

LOUIS:

That is for others to judge. I am pleased we helped to make the world safer.

MARIE:

Louis, you did far more than that. Think of your work with vaccines.

JONTY:

What about cholera? I gather you got the germ of an idea from an English doctor called John Snow? 'Germ of an idea', ha! Did you see what I did there?

LOUIS:

Ah yes, I read about John Snow's discovery and that got me thinking. It was like this...

MISH:

Sorry to interrupt, but before you say any more,

I can tell you that we've managed to bring John Snow here tonight on Eurostar from Brompton Cemetery in London. Please welcome the ghost of John Snow...
(He enters)

MARIE:

Oh, Doctor Snow, how we admired your work. You weren't just Queen Victoria's doctor. You also proved how cholera spread. That was music to our ears.

JOHN:

I'm delighted to join you. Yes, in 1854 we had a major cholera epidemic in London with many deaths. At that time doctors thought it spread in 'smelly air' but I disagreed. It was my belief that the disease spread in dirty water. If people drink it, they get severe diarrhoea and vomiting. They can soon die.

LOUIS:

You are so right, John. And you proved how it spread once and for all.

JOHN:

I discovered that the London cholera outbreak came from a single well in Soho. A mother washed a nappy at a water pump and contaminated the water supply. I had the pump removed and the cholera stopped immediately. So you see, disease didn't come from 'bad air' at all. That was just 'miasma nonsense'.

MISH:

Although you died in 1858, when Louis was developing Pasteurisation as a way to make liquids safe, you both believed in 'germ theory' and your work changed health, hygiene and the control of cholera.

LOUIS:

Three years after John's death, I announced my germ theory to the world. I'm so delighted to meet you at last – although I won't shake your hand, just in case.

JOHN:

I thought French people greeted each other with kisses?

MARIE:

Not in our house we don't. It's far too dangerous.

JONTY:

By the way, Doctor Snow, you might like to know how Louis Pasteur went on to develop a vaccine for cholera in chickens.

JOHN:

A vaccine? How fascinating. You must tell me all about that.

MISH:

Well, he doesn't have to. If you look at that giant plasma screen, coming up next is what happened ten years after you died at the age of 45. That's when Louis Pasteur found a way to prevent cholera killing chickens.

MARIE:

I helped as well, you know...

Foul times to fowl times

BAD TIMES HIT THE PASTEURS IN 1868.

WE'VE LOST THREE OF OUR CHILDREN IN THE LAST FEW YEARS. DON'T LET ME LOSE YOU, LOUIS.

I'VE JUST BEEN OVERWORKING, THAT'S ALL.

AT THE AGE OF 45, LOUIS IS LEFT PARALYSED ON HIS LEFT SIDE BY A STROKE.

BUT LOOK AT THE COST TO YOUR HEALTH.

I WON'T LET THIS BEAT ME. MY BEST WORK IS YET TO COME.

MAMA, GREAT ACHIEVEMENTS ALWAYS COME AT A COST. YOU CAN'T MAKE AN OMELETTE WITHOUT BREAKING EGGS.

QUEL DOMMAGE! THIS IS A JOB FOR SUPER-LOUIS.

TALKING OF EGGS... CHICKENS ARE HAVING A FOWL TIME, TOO.

Ghosts reunited

MISH:

Welcome back to the *Live from the Crypt* sofa, where we're delighted to have Louis and Marie Pasteur still with us and about to meet a couple more ghosts who are coming to join us.

JONTY:

Yes, this is 'Ghosts reunited', where we bring together ghosts who haven't met for a while,

which could make for an interesting encounter. Fortunately, we have programmed our software to translate French and German into English for our viewers.

MARIE:

German? Did you say German? We didn't get on with Germany. Beware of any country with a GERM in it.

LOUIS:

I hope you're not talking about my chief rival? We didn't like each other.

JONTY:

Well, we've managed to hunt him down, or should I say 'haunt him down'.

MISH:

And he's just arrived after a six-hour train journey from Baden-Baden where he lays in rest in the mausoleum at the Robert Koch Institute...

MARIE:

Pah – send him back. He never liked us.

JONTY:

Then maybe this is the time to put the record straight. He wanted to come and congratulate you and thank you for inspiring a lot of his work. After all, the names of Koch and Pasteur are giants of 19th century epidemiology. That's the study of epidemics, diseases and health, by the way.

MARIE:

We still don't like him.

LOUIS:

We'd better hear what he has to say. He was at least twenty years younger than me so he might have lived to discover new things. He was clever, I'll give him that.

ROBERT:

(Enters in mask, gown, surgical gloves and goggles.) Good evening. Long time, no see.

MARIE:

(Under breath) Thank goodness.

LOUIS:

You seem to have aged since I saw you last, Robert.

ROBERT:

That's because I'm dead, Louis. I have to admit it was your ideas about germs that first inspired me to create the science of bacteriology. My methods were much more thorough than yours and I went on to be the first scientist to identify the bacteria that causes anthrax, TB and human cholera.

I WAS AWARDED THE NOBEL PRIZE FOR MEDICINE IN 1905.

MARIE:

Pah, it was Louis who worked on successful vaccines. Much more useful.

LOUIS:

I read about your work, Robert, and it spurred me on to do better, seeing as our countries were at war. Your government gave you a team of scientists to assist you, so then I got our government to back me. I ran my own institute.

ROBERT:

I'll have you know, I set up the Robert Koch Institute in 1891. So there.

LOUIS:

Really? I set mine up three years before yours. So there.

MISH:

So let's all agree that in the 1880s and 1890s you both made great progress in identifying bacteria that caused disease and in developing vaccines.

MARIE:

Louis developed more vaccines.

ROBERT:

But I worked more to protect communities with better hygiene and public health. After all, I was a trained medical doctor, Louis wasn't. So there.

LOUIS:

Oh dear, this is like 1882 all over again. That's when you came to my lecture and got all stroppy at what I said.

ROBERT:

That's because you were talking rubbish.

MARIE:

No, Louis was talking French. The translator messed up and it all came out wrong in German. That's why you got all bolshie.

JONTY:

Maybe I can just come in here and try to calm things down. Let's talk about cholera for a moment. You both believed it spread in dirty water...

ROBERT:

Of course. I made rules about hygiene and water supply to stop the disease spreading. In fact, and I don't like to boast, I won a prize of 100,000 German marks for my work on cholera. So there.

LOUIS:

Really? I think you'll find that it was a Spanish admirer of mine called Jaime Ferrán who was the first scientist to create a human cholera vaccine. So there.

MARIE:

Nice one, Lou! You tell him.

MISH:

Whilst on the subject of cholera, we happen to have another great German scientist ghost with us tonight. Please welcome Max Von Pettenkofer.

MAX:

(Enters in white lab coat, carrying a glass of muddy liquid.) Good evening.

ROBERT:

Oh no, not him!

JONTY:

Were you another of Robert Koch's rivals, Max?

MAX:

I guess so. I did a lot of work to develop proper hygiene and sewers in the German city of Munich, which was full of cholera before I got rid of it.

THEY CALLED ME THE FATHER OF HYGIENE, DESPITE MY GRUBBY BEARD.

ROBERT:

Ha, tell them the rest, Max. You were so wrong about the cause of cholera.

MAX:

Nonsense. I disagreed with John Snow, and then you, as you said cholera spread in water. I said it was in the soil. Cholera is in the ground, you see.

ROBERT:

So, to prove you wrong, I sent you a glass of filthy water to drink.

MAX:

Yes, and I've brought it with me. Look, it's just a bit muddy, that's all.

ROBERT:

It's got cholera in it. And I dared you to drink it.

MAX:

No problem. I proved you wrong – look...
(Drinks the whole glass.)

LOUIS:

That really isn't a good idea.

MARIE:

Did you survive?

MAX:

Of course. I'm a great German scientist after all.

ROBERT:

But it didn't do you any good, did it?

MAX:

True. *(Pulls face.)*
Excuse me... I need the bathroom. *(Rushes out.)*

ROBERT:

He did recover but it ruined his weekend. Louis and I were right all along. I now call him Max Von Petten-cough-up!

JONTY:

Brilliant – we can finish our chat in perfect agreement and harmony after all.

MARIE:

Not exactly.

MISH:

We would just like to warn viewers not to try Max Von Pettenkofer's experiment at home. Drinking cholera can seriously damage your health.

JONTY:

And your toilet. If you have been affected by issues raised in this programme, it'll be nothing like as bad as Max is being affected right now. We apologise for the horrible noises coming from the bathroom down the corridor.

MISH:

Which all goes to prove that even ghosts have to avoid drinking germs.

JONTY:

So, on that bombshell, we leave 'Ghosts reunited' and return to the giant plasma screen for a dramatic storyboard. We must warn viewers there are disturbing images from the outset...

Research with bite

DURING THE 1880s, LOUIS PASTEUR AND HIS TEAM ARE BUSY STUDYING RABIES.

FIRSTLY, TAKE A RABBIT WITH RABIES AND LOOK INSIDE ITS BRAIN AND SPINE.

WE'LL INJECT A RABID RABBIT'S TISSUE INTO A DOG.

YOU'VE GOT TO HELP ME. MY BOY HAS BEEN ATTACKED BY A DOG WITH RABIES.

AND WE'D BE ABLE TO MAKE A VACCINE. IF NOT, WE'RE STUMPED.

IF THE DOG DOESN'T CATCH THE DISEASE, IT MIGHT DEVELOP RESISTANCE TO IT.

IN 1885, MADAME MEISTER ARRIVES AT PASTEUR'S LABORATORY.

130

Interview with the Ghost of Louis Pasteur

131

JOSEPH NEVER DEVELOPS RABIES. THE TREATMENT WORKS!

TWO MONTHS LATER, A 15-YEAR-OLD SHEPHERD ARRIVES AT THE LABORATORY.

A MAD DOG RAN AT US SO I JUMPED ON IT TO LET THE OTHER SHEPHERDS ESCAPE. IT BIT ME BIG TIME. OUCH.

HE'LL DIE FROM RABIES IF WE DON'T TRY OUR NEW VACCINE.

JEAN-BAPTISTE NEVER DEVELOPS RABIES. THE TREATMENT DEFINITELY WORKS!

LOUIS TRIES HIS TREATMENT ON JEAN-BAPTISTE JUPILLE.

LOUIS PASTEUR IS NATIONAL HERO

LOUIS PASTEUR PUBLISHES HIS RESULTS AND SETS UP A RABIES TREATMENT RESEARCH CENTRE.

133

Spin the news

ALEEMA:

And now it's 'Spin the News', where I spin a dial for the news headlines from a mystery year *(spins a dial which stops at 1881)*. 1881. It was a time of great creativity in Paris, with French impressionist painters such as Renoir, Cézanne and Monet causing a stir. But what might that year have to do with science and spinning a yarn, I wonder?

LOUIS:

Has your question got anything to do with silk or wool?

MARIE:

Was it the year you injected all those sheep, Louis? *(Enter Émile Roux.)*

ÉMILE:

I think you'll find it was me who did all that. It was the year we won the prize.

LOUIS:

Émile! It's great to see you.

ALEEMA:

Erm, we weren't expecting anyone else. How did you get in here? Who are you?

MARIE:

It's Émile Roux – he lives here. At least, he had an apartment here after us.

ÉMILE:

I worked with Louis for years. My tomb is just outside here in the garden.

ALEEMA:

So what do you remember about the year 1881?

Interview with the Ghost of Louis Pasteur

ÉMILE:

I was a young scientist aged 28 years, some thirty years younger than Louis. It was the year he was awarded the Grand Cross of the Legion of Honour.

MARIE:

There's no higher honour – all for his anthrax experiments with sheep.

ÉMILE:

But Louis wouldn't accept the award alone. He insisted that Charles Chamberland and I also received the award. Louis took the blue ribbon and we took the red. It was very generous of him.

LOUIS:

Well, it was you on your own who inoculated all the sheep, Émile.

ALEEMA:

Is it true you were challenged to a public test of your anthrax vaccine?

MARIE:

Other scientists couldn't believe Louis had found a way to stop anthrax spreading.

ÉMILE:

We used fifty sheep in the test. I inoculated twenty-five with the vaccine.

LOUIS:

They were then injected with deadly anthrax, along with twenty-five others.

ÉMILE:

Those that were not inoculated died within two days. The group I inoculated had no ill effects whatsoever.

MARIE:

The judge described them as 'frolicking in perfect health' and they proved Louis hadn't exaggerated the powers of his vaccine. Clever Louis!

ÉMILE:

The Times newspaper in Britain called Louis 'one of the scientific glories of France'. There was an

English joke, but it doesn't work in French. Here goes: 'Louis Pasteur injected twenty sick sheep. Nineteen died. How many were left?'

ALEEMA:

Easy. There were six left. Twenty-six take away nineteen is six.

ÉMILE:

Aha! I didn't say he injected twenty-SIX sheep but twenty SICK sheep. That always fools people. Try that teaser on your friends and see!

LOUIS:

You might wonder how we made the first anthrax vaccine. Basically, we got some anthrax organisms and weakened them with a kind of disinfectant called carbolic acid. My friend in England was a surgeon and he began using carbolic acid to kill germs in hospitals. He was dead keen about my germ theory.

ÉMILE:

Now he's just dead.

MARIE:

You may have heard of the great Joseph Lister. He operated on Queen Victoria and saved many lives, just by using antiseptic to keep hospitals clean.

LOUIS:

Joseph and I had a great meeting in 1881. I went to a medical conference in London and we excitedly shared with each other our research on carbolic acid.

ALEEMA:

Well, it just so happens we can talk to him now. Watch the plasma screen as we go live by satellite to Hampstead Cemetery in London, to meet the ghost of Joseph Lister...

JOSEPH:

Hello, it's great to be with you, Louis and friends. How are you, Louis?

LOUIS:

Fine, Joseph. Dead but fine. I'm only five years older than you but you look much fitter. It must be all that clean living surrounded by antiseptics!

JOSEPH:

That's thanks to you, Louis. I learned all about germs from your work on rotten food and diseases. I experimented with chemicals to clean my patients' festering wounds. When I used sterile instruments and dressings, so many more patients survived. Together, we changed the world of medicine, Louis.

MARIE:

They call you 'the father of modern surgery' and Louis 'the father of microbiology'.

LOUIS:

You helped me prove to the world that microscopic organisms play such a huge part in infectious disease. Until then, few scientists believed us.

JOSEPH:

And when we met in 1881, you were so excited about your work on chicken cholera vaccine, that we talked forever and kept writing to each other about our experiments. Great times. I was very sad when you died, Louis – and you, Marie – fifteen years later. I managed to keep going until

I was 84. Unlike you, I don't suppose anyone even knows my name now.

ALEEMA:

They named a mouthwash after you, Dr Lister. In World War One they put on the bottle: 'Kills germs that cause bad breath.'

JOSEPH:

I think I'd rather have my name on bottles of milk, like my friend Louis Pasteur!

EMILE:

You could always team up and create super-antiseptic milk that doubles as a mouthwash? With that on your cornflakes, you wouldn't need to clean your teeth after breakfast!

ALEEMA:

Probably not your best idea, Émile. To our younger viewers: please don't try this at home!

ÉMILE:

Or on biscuit breakfast cereal at 8 o'clock – known in France as Huit Heures Bics!

ALEEMA:

On that dreadful pun, we come to the end of 'Spin the Year'. I'd like to thank all of our guests for sharing their memories. So from all of us here, it's now goodnight.

ALL:

Goodnight.

ALEEMA:

There's just time to return to the giant plasma screen for the last storyboard, telling us about the final years of the great Louis Pasteur. Keep watching, as we go back to the 1890s and relive far more than the end of a century...

The last years

Interview with the Ghost of LOUIS PASTEUR

And finally

MISH:

You join us back on the *Live from the Crypt* sofa now that all of our ghostly guests have departed and it's a bit quiet, I must say...

JONTY:

Ghostly quiet, Mish. But we're not quite ready to say a final goodnight, as we have one last ghost guest coming to us on the screen.

MISH:

Yes – and finally, we are delighted to welcome by satellite-link from London, in the northern aisle at the east end of the Crypt of St Paul's Cathedral, the Nobel Prize-winning discoverer of the antibiotic Penicillin: Sir Alexander Fleming.

JONTY:

Can you hear us, Sir Alexander?

ALEXANDER:

Indeed I can. It's good to be with you. After all, Louis Pasteur is a hero of mine.

MISH:

And I'm sure he would have been amazed by what you did in the 1920s when you were working on harmful bacteria and discovered something by accident.

ALEXANDER:

Exactly. When I woke up on 28th September 1928, I had no idea I would change medicine forever by discovering the world's first antibiotic. I'd left a dish of nasty bacteria in a dish when I went on holiday. Some mould got into it without my knowledge and began killing the bacteria. Penicillin was born!

JONTY:

Did you realise what you'd discovered?

ALEXANDER:

It took a while – in fact, it wasn't until the 1940s that other scientists and I began to mass-produce Penicillin and make it into the medicine that has saved millions of lives. Antibiotics have been fighting infections ever since.

MISH:

If only Louis Pasteur knew that a type of fungi could kill harmful germs.

ALEXANDER:

He once said, 'Chance favours only the prepared mind'. I guess a lot of luck was involved but fortunately we were prepared to think of all the possibilities. Louis Pasteur was absolutely right, of course.

JONTY:

The spooky part about all this is that the date you made your discovery was exactly 33 years to the day Louis Pasteur died and 18 to the day Marie died. So 28th September should be known as International Germ Day.

MISH:

It's also World Rabies Day. What a great day to celebrate discoveries in medical science. Maybe we can talk to you again on that date, Sir Alexander?

ALEXANDER:

I'd be delighted. I'll write it in my diary. Why don't we all meet up again for a party on 28th September 2028 – the 100th anniversary of Penicillin?

JONTY:

It's a date. I'll bring the blue cheese sandwiches. As that's a kind of mould, it's just right for a Penicillin celebration!

MISH:

Not really, Jonty. We should quickly move on. We'll say 'goodbye' to Alexander Fleming until next time, while we look at some of the tweets and texts coming in.

JONTY:

Yes, we've just received a few tweets from viewers. The first is from a Mike Robe who writes: 'Pasteur's enthusiasm for diseases must have been truly infectious.'

MISH:

And an Ann Thrax says: 'Your video clip about rabies has just gone viral.'

JONTY:

Here's a text from Enoch Yewlate, who states: 'All this stuff about vaccines and disease – I just don't get it. I guess I'm measly confused.'

MISH:

And very finally, a text from Penny Sillin who says: 'Fleming was a man of great culture and a fun guy who certainly broke the mould.'

JONTY:

OK, that's enough of all that nonsense. Our time is up, so all that remains is for us to go back to Larna who is right at the Pasteur tomb itself...

LARNA:

That's right, Jonty. Louis and Marie have just
returned here and they've invited us back on 27th
December 2022 for Louis Pasteur's 200th birthday.
He said there'll be plenty of pasteurised milk and
well-fermented beer and wine. So, join us then for
'Party from the Crypt'. Until then, it's goodnight
from us all at the Pasteur Institute in Paris and
from all our ghostly guests. Goodnight!

Family tree

JEAN-JOSEPH PASTEUR
1791–1865

JEANNE-ETIENNE ROQUI
1793–1848

JEAN
1816–1817

JEANNE ANTOINE
1818–1880

JOSEPHINE
1825–1850

JEANNE
1850–1859

JEAN-BAPTISTE
1851–1908

CÉCILE
1853–1866

CAMILLE
1880–1927

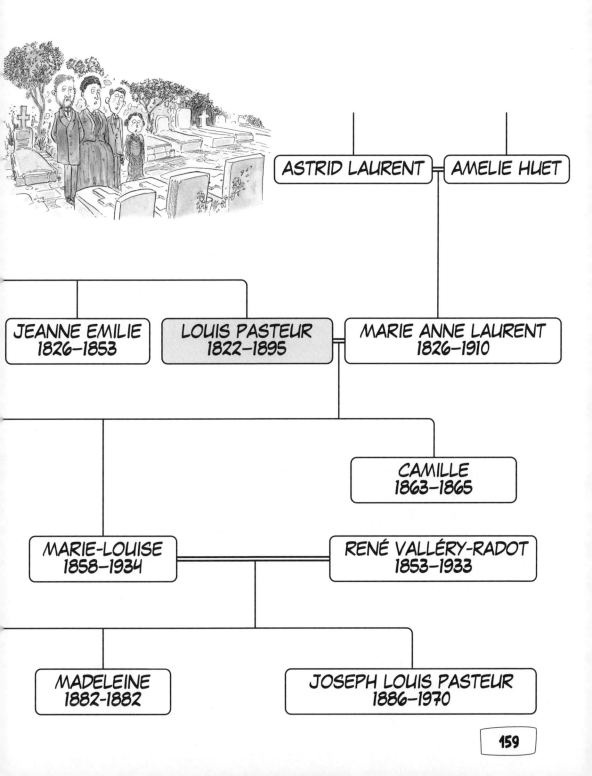

ASTRID LAURENT — AMELIE HUET

JEANNE EMILIE
1826–1853

LOUIS PASTEUR
1822–1895

MARIE ANNE LAURENT
1826–1910

CAMILLE
1863–1865

MARIE-LOUISE
1858–1934

RENÉ VALLÉRY-RADOT
1853–1933

MADELEINE
1882-1882

JOSEPH LOUIS PASTEUR
1886–1970

Timeline

1822

27th December – Louis Pasteur is born in Dole, France.

1827

Louis's father starts a tannery in Arbois.

1831

Louis starts studying at a primary school called Le College d'Arbois. He witnesses a child attacked by a rabid dog and is affected by the horror.

1844

He enters École normale supérieure, Paris.

1848:

He becomes a chemistry professor at the University of Strasbourg.

Interview with the Ghost of LOUIS PASTEUR

1849

He marries Marie Laurent, the university rector's daughter.

1850

Louis and Marie's first child, Jeanne, is born.

1851

Louis and Marie's second child, Jean-Baptiste, is born.

1853

Louis and Marie's third child, Cécile, is born.

1854

Louis becomes Dean of Faculty of Sciences at the University of Lille.

1855

He begins research into fermentation.

1857

He goes to Paris as Director of Science Studies of the École normale supérieure.

1858

Louis and Marie's fourth child, Marie Louise, is born.

1859

Louis' daughter, Jeanne, dies at the age of 9.

1861

Louis publishes his work on germ theory about airborne microbes and disease.

1862

He completes his pasteurisation tests.

1863

Louis and Marie's fifth child, Camille, is born.

1865

Their daughter Camille dies.

1866

Their daughter Cécile dies.

1867

Joseph Lister publishes 'On The Antiseptic Principle in the Practice of Surgery', based partly on Pasteur's work on germs.

1868

Louis suffers a stroke, leaving his left side paralysed.

1870s

Louis and Robert Koch develop the germ theory of disease further.

1876

Louis publishes important findings about fermentation: 'Studies on Beer' (10 years after his 'Studies on Wine').

1878/9

He develops a vaccine for cholera in chickens.

1881

He successfully demonstrates an anthrax vaccine.

1885

He demonstrates a rabies vaccine using young Joseph Meister.

1887

He establishes the Pasteur Institute in Paris.

1895

Louis is awarded the Leeuwenhoek Medal for services to microbiology.

1895

Louis Pasteur dies after a stroke, aged 72 years, on 28th September.

1910

Marie Pasteur dies aged 84 on 28th September – exactly 15 years after Louis.

Quiz - Qui veut gagner des millions?
(Who wants to be a French franc millionaire?)

Can you answer all the questions to win one million French francs?

(You can play this quiz on your own or with a contestant, a question-host and an audience.)

Interview with the Ghost of LOUIS PASTEUR

1. For 100 francs – Louis Pasteur was born in eastern France, near to which country?
a) England.
b) Germany.
c) Spain.
d) Australia.

2. For 200 francs – Who was Louis Pasteur buried with?
a) Napoleon.
b) Émile.
c) Marie.
d) Rabbits.

3. For 300 francs – When he was at school, Louis was best at which subjects?
a) Art and singing.
b) Football and rugby.
c) Cooking and childcare.
d) Chasing girls.

4. For 500 francs – Pasteur proved scientists who thought that diseases appeared from nowhere wrong. This was known as
a) Spontaneous putrefaction.
b) Scandalous pantrification.
c) Instantaneous regurgitation.
d) Spontaneous generation.

5. For 1,000 francs – Which of these images does NOT appear inside Louis Pasteur's crypt?
a) Bubbling test tubes .
b) Snarling dogs.
c) Grazing sheep.
d) Hopping rabbits.

6. For 2,000 francs – Which of these is NOT a symptom of rabies?
a) Frothing at the mouth.
b) Fear of water and drinking.
c) Fear of spiders.
d) Fever and shivering.

7. For 4,000 francs – Where does the word vaccination come from?
a) Vacuum (sucking out disease).
b) Vacca (Latin for cow).
c) Vacation (when germs spread most).
d) Vacant (empty of infected cells).

8. For 8,000 francs – What was 'Miasma Theory' that Louis Pasteur disproved?
a) Disease caused by bad smells.
b) Disease caused by sour milk.
c) Disease caused by dirty blood.
d) Disease caused by fleas.

9. For 16,000 francs – What is Pasteurisation?
a) Spraying pasture to kill bugs.
b) Boiling pasta to kill yeast.
c) Sterilising meat paste with bleach.
d) Heating liquids to kill germs.

10. For 32,000 francs – Which of these creatures did Louis Pasteur NOT study for research into diseases?
a) Maggots.
b) Silkworms.
c) Rabbits.
d) Chickens.

Interview with the Ghost of LOUIS PASTEUR

11. For 64,000 francs – How many of Louis and Marie Pasteur's five children survived to become adults?
a) 1.
b) 2.
c) 3.
d) 4.

12. For 125,000 francs – What was the name of the boy on whom Louis Pasteur tested a vaccine for rabies?
a) James Phipps.
b) Joseph Jupille.
c) Joseph Meister.
d) Jean-Baptiste Bigo.

13. For 250,000 francs – Which of these scientists did NOT work with Louis Pasteur?
a) Max Von Pettenkofer.
b) Marie Pasteur.
c) Charles Chamberland.
d) Émile Roux.

14. For 500,000 francs – In 1881 Louis Pasteur and his team were awarded the Grand Cross of the Legion of Honour. Why?
a) For developing Pasteurisation.
b) For saving the French silk industry.
c) For researching into cholera.
d) For developing an anthrax vaccine.

15. For 1 million francs – When is World Rabies Day?
a) 27th December
b) 28th September
c) 29th October
d) 30th November

The franc was the currency in France at the time of Louis Pasteur. It was replaced by the Euro in 1999. However many Francs you just won... they are now totally worthless. Unlucky!

ANSWERS:
1 (B) 2 (C) 3 (A) 4 (D) 5 (A)
6 (C) 7 (B) 8 (A) 9 (D) 10 (A) 11 (B)
12 (C) 13 (A) 14 (D) 15 (B)

Glossary

ANTHRAX
An infectious and often deadly disease (mainly in cattle and sheep) caused by a bacterium. It is also dangerous to humans.

BACTERIOLOGY
Science that deals with bacteria and their effects on living things.

BOTULISM & SALMONELLA

Food poisoning caused by eating types of 'bad bacteria'.

EPIDEMIC

An outbreak of disease that spreads to many people in one area.

EPIDEMIOLOGY

Medical science that deals with the distribution and control of disease.

FERMENT

The chemical breakdown of a substance due to the action of microscopic organisms (like the souring of milk).

IMMUNOLOGY

Science dealing with immunity (the body's resistance) to infectious disease.

MIASMA

An unpleasant or unhealthy smell or vapour.

MICROBIOLOGY

A branch of science concerned with microscopic forms of life (microbes such as bacteria and viruses).

PASTEURISATION

The process discovered by Louis Pasteur of heating a liquid (like milk) and keeping it at that temperature long enough to kill harmful bacteria and then cooling it quickly without causing a major change in its chemical composition.

In the classroom

10 TITLES IN CHRONOLOGICAL ORDER:

TUTANKHAMUN
ANCIENT EGYPT AND HOWARD CARTER'S 1922 DISCOVERIES.

QIN SHI HUANG
ANCIENT CHINA AND THE TERRACOTTA ARMY DISCOVERY OF 1974.

ROMAN EMPERORS
ANCIENT ROME AND THE FIRST 5 NOTORIOUS EMPERORS AFTER JULIUS CAESAR.

HENRY VIII
TUDOR ENGLAND AND THE TURBULENT TRIALS OF KING AND COUNTRY.

PIRATES
17TH & 18TH CENTURY SWASHBUCKLING ON THE HIGH SEAS AND THE CARIBBEAN.

QUEEN VICTORIA
THE LIFE AND TIMES OF AN ENIGMATIC QUEEN AND HER VICTORIAN WORLD.

LOUIS PASTEUR
THE AGE OF SCIENTIFIC DISCOVERY: DISEASE, GERM THEORY AND HYGIENE.

SPARKY INVENTORS
THE AGE OF ELECTRICITY PIONEERS; FROM THOMAS EDISON TO NIKOLA TESLA.

WOMEN DOCTORS AND MEDICAL PIONEERS
MARIE CURIE AND THE FIRST WOMEN NOBEL PRIZE-WINNERS.

TITANIC
THE FAMOUS TRAGEDY TOLD BY THOSE WHO WERE THERE.

(ARRANGING THE BOOKS IN ORDER COULD BE AN ACTIVITY IN ITSELF!)

Each of these books is primarily for solitary reading, but they have also been designed with the option for groups to read and perform together as a play at school, home or anywhere else.

A whole class can be included, or smaller groups if individuals take on several parts. There are plenty of flexible possibilities to involve as many or as few as required.

The books can be broken up into their various scenes for reading, performing or recording on video or audio equipment separately, simultaneously or with everyone together. On the other hand, one solitary individual could, with different voices, record scenes alone. The ultimate aim is that all who read or perform should be entertained, informed, engaged and encouraged to enjoy plenty of imaginative factual fun.

Ideas for performance

As well as the 20 or so character parts in each book, there is plenty of scope for extra roles for both performers and creators behind the scenes.

Potential extra roles

FACT-CHECKER(S)

Throughout the script, various bizarre facts with unusual information appear. Occasionally a flag/banner could pop up saying 'That's TRUE!' (Maybe with an added comment such as 'Yes, they really did eat x'.) Someone could verify such facts or add an extra detail, then be responsible for holding up the sign at the appropriate time in the show.

CONTESTANTS

A few willing volunteers to sit the final quiz could swot up on information before sitting in the hotseat. If a contestant chooses the wrong answer, a replacement volunteer can take over from where they left off. Four lifelines are available: 50-50 (2 wrong answers removed), ask the host, ask the audience and ask a friend.

DIRECTOR

A suitable person will need to take control of fitting everything together, making decisions and directing the cast (as well as taking the blame!)

SOUND EFFECTS

Someone could be responsible for recording/playing appropriate sound effects, TV jingles and songs/music between scenes or to link sections. Anyone so inspired and skilled could adapt the comic strip sequences for PowerPoint (or some such) visual presentation for showing on screen.

QUIZ HOST

The questioner can read out each question followed by the four possible answers, or a PowerPoint slide can be prepared for showing each question. A second slide can also be prepared with two wrong answers omitted, should the contestant ask for the 50-50 option. The questioner shouldn't see the answer until the contestant says 'final answer', particularly if the 'ask the host' lifeline has been chosen. If the 'ask the audience' lifeline is chosen, the host asks everyone to vote for each answer in turn by raising a hand (voting only once!). After counting the votes for each question, the host repeats the figures to the contestant. If the 'ask a friend' lifeline is used, the contestant will already have chosen someone in the audience to ask. The host invites the friend to give an answer, checks if they are correct and announces the result.

Additional activities

CHARACTER CARDS

All the characters in the book (whether a genuine historical character or from the TV team) can be summarised on a card with simple headings, scores and personality characteristics. These can then be discussed, displayed or even 'played' if players compare their cards or devise 'Top Trump'-style activities. Lists of character traits/ adjectives can be added, with students having to justify why they have chosen their descriptions. Some examples follow:

CHARACTER CARD

NAME:

DATES: COUNTRY:

STRENGTH	
WEAKNESS	
SKILL	
BIG MOMENT	
QUOTE	

CALM	SILLY	GRUMPY	ANGRY
CHALLENGING	CHEERFUL	POMPOUS	CLUMSY
CONFIDENT	MISERABLE	TENSE	DULL
GOOD-NATURED	CAPABLE	NERVOUS	LAZY
WISE	CHARMING	SELFISH	SHY
DREAMY	ENTHUSIASTIC	CARING	SCARY
STUBBORN	KIND	CLEVER	LIVELY
ANXIOUS	WITTY	FRIENDLY	PATIENT
CRUEL	INTENSE	SENSITIVE	SLEEPY
GLOOMY	TOUGH	ARGUMENTATIVE	GIGGLY
MOODY	DOMINEERING	SARCASTIC	BORED

TIMELINE TEASER

This could be a puzzle for individuals/pairs or a timed group competition. It would feature the timeline at the back of the book. A photocopy with a few blanks, together with a choice of answers displayed elsewhere, should keep everyone happily amused, engaged and even enraged! This offers a great way of consolidating understanding of the context of the events in the book.

MATCH THE MEANING

Chopping up a copy of the glossary provides a fun way for students to match words with their definitions, helping to learn key vocabulary and ideas.

COMMERCIAL BREAK

How about developing the advertisements from the commercial break with extra jingles, cheesy ad-talk, dialogue, sketches, slogans and even a few puppets thrown in the mix?

Index

Published in Great Britain in MMXXI by
Book House, an imprint of
The Salariya Book Company Ltd
25 Marlborough Place, Brighton BN1 1UB
www.salariya.com

ISBN: 978-1-913337-78-0

SCRIBO   BOOK HOUSE   SCRIBBLERS

1 3 5 7 9 8 6 4 2

A CIP catalogue record for this book is available
from the British Library.

Printed and bound in Malta.

Author: John Townsend
Illustrator: Rory Walker
Editor: Nick Pierce

Visit
www.salariya.com
for our online catalogue and
free fun stuff.

PAPER FROM
SUSTAINABLE
FORESTS